I0755013

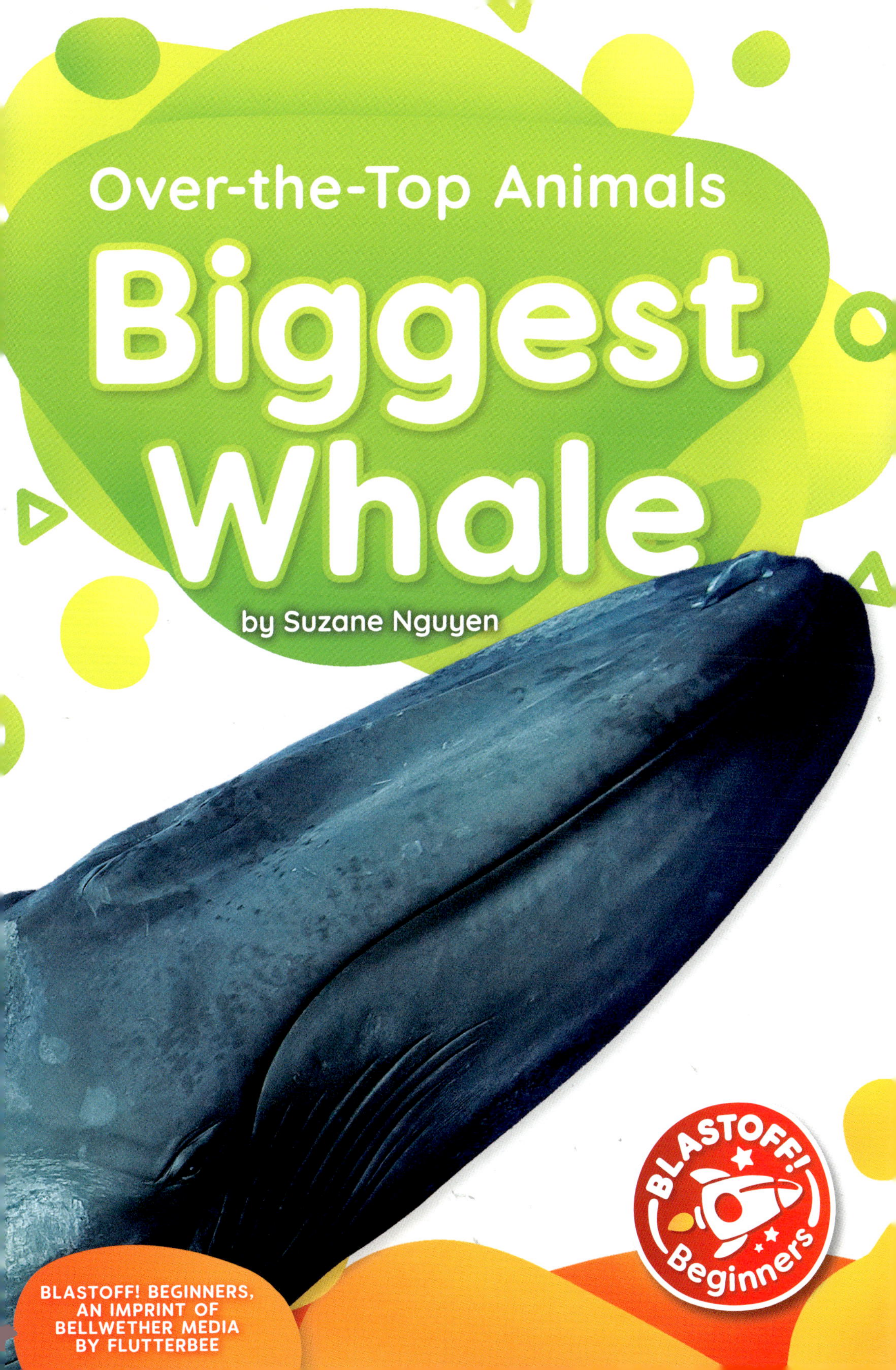
Over-the-Top Animals
Biggest Whale
by Suzane Nguyen
BLASTOFF! Beginners
BLASTOFF! BEGINNERS, AN IMPRINT OF BELLWETHER MEDIA BY FLUTTERBEE

Blastoff! Beginners are developed by literacy experts and educators to meet the needs of early readers. These engaging informational texts support young children as they begin reading about their world. Through simple language and high frequency words paired with crisp, colorful photos, Blastoff! Beginners launch young readers into the universe of independent reading.

Sight Words in This Book

a	as	eat	it	their
an	big	go	of	them
and	blue	have	on	they
are	by	help	the	too

This edition first published in 2027 by Bellwether Media, Inc.

For information regarding permission, write to Bellwether Media, Inc., Attention: Permissions Department, 3500 American Blvd W, Suite 150, Bloomington, MN 55431.

Library of Congress Cataloging-in-Publication Data is available at www.loc.gov or upon request from the publisher.

ISBN: 9798893049961 (hardcover)
ISBN: 9798898801380 (ebook)

Editor: Betsy Rathburn   Designer: Laura Sowers

Table of Contents

A blue whale
swims by.
It flips its big tail!

The Biggest Whale

Blue whales are the biggest **mammals** on Earth!

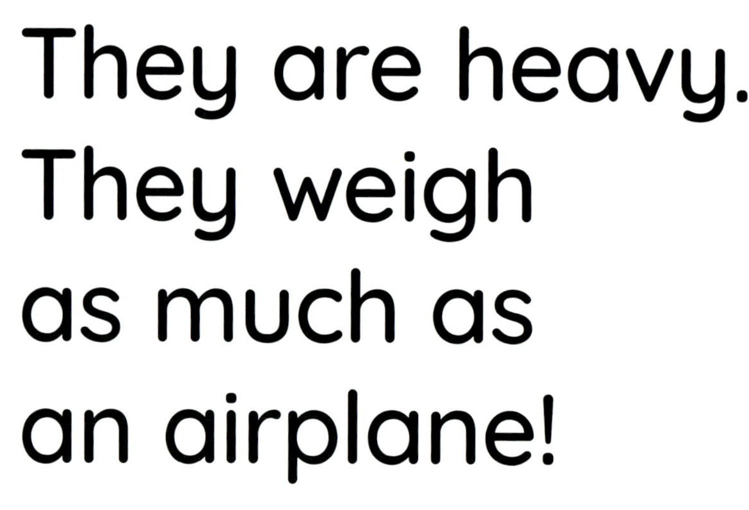

They are heavy.
They weigh
as much as
an airplane!

They have big mouths. Their **baleen** traps food.

They have big fins. Their tails are big too.

fin

Huge Swimmers

Blue whales have a lot of **blubber**. It keeps them warm.

They eat tiny **krill**. Big mouths help them eat a lot!

krill

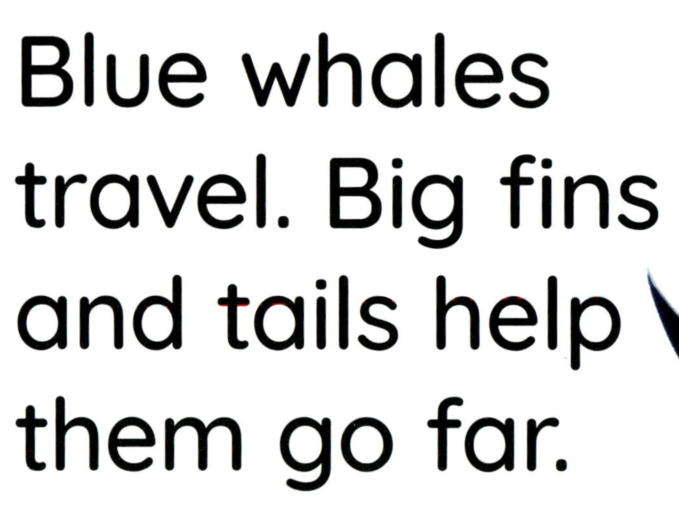

Blue whales travel. Big fins and tails help them go far.

Blue whales
rule the ocean.
Watch them go!

The Biggest Whale

Body Parts

Why Are They Big?

keep warm

eat a lot of krill

travel far

Glossary

baleen

hard parts that catch food in the mouths of whales

blubber

body fat that keeps whales warm

krill

small, shrimplike sea animals

mammals

warm-blooded animals that have hair and feed their young milk

To Learn More

ON THE WEB

FACTSURFER

Factsurfer.com gives you a safe, fun way to find more information.

1. Go to www.factsurfer.com.
2. Enter "biggest whale" into the search box and click 🔍.
3. Select your book cover to see a list of related content.

Index

The images in this book are reproduced through the courtesy of: WaterFrame/ Alamy Stock Photo, front cover, pp. 12-13, 23 (blubber); Gerald Corsi, p. 3; Flip Nicklin/ Minden Pictures/ SuperStock, pp. 4-5; Nature Picture Library/ Alamy Stock Photo, pp. 6-7, 8-9, 10-11, 16-17, 18-19, 22 (keep warm), 22 (eat a lot of krill); Malcolm Schuyl/ Alamy Stock Photo, pp. 10, 23 (baleen); max-Photography, p. 12; Darin Sakdatorn, pp. 14-15; RLS Photo, p. 16; YamMo, pp. 20-21; Andrew Sutton, p. 22; Scubazoo/ Science Faction/ SuperStock, p. 22 (travel far); Tarpan, p. 23 (krill); blickwinkel/ Alamy Stock Photo, p. 23 (mammals).